To:

From:

Date:

D0616318

© 2009 by Barbour Publishing, Inc.

ISBN 978-1-63058-723-9

Scripture quotations marked KJV are taken from the King James Version of the Bible.

Scripture quotations marked NIV are taken from the HOLY BIBLE, NEW INTERNATIONAL VERSION®. NIV®. Copyright © 1973, 1978, 1984, 2011 by Biblia, Inc™. Used by permission. All rights reserved worldwide.

Scripture quotations marked MSG are from *THE MESSAGE.* Copyright © 1993, 1994, 1995, 1996, 2000, 2001, 2002 by Eugene H. Peterson. Used by permission of NavPress Publishing Group.

Scripture quotations marked NLT are taken from the Holy Bible, New Living Translation, copyright © 1996, 2004, 2007, 2013 by Tyndale House Foundation. Used by permission of Tyndale House Publishers, Inc., Carol Stream, Illinois 60188. All rights reserved.

Published by DayMaker, an imprint of Barbour Publishing, Inc., P.O. Box 719, Uhrichsville, Ohio 44683, www.barbourbooks.com

*Our mission is to publish and distribute inspirational products offering exceptional value and biblical encouragement to the masses.*

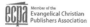
Member of the
Evangelical Christian
Publishers Association

Printed in China.

# Little
# Whispers of
# Wisdom

## *for*
## *Women*

DAYMAKER™
An Imprint of Barbour Publishing, Inc.

Joy is prayer.
Joy is strength. Joy is love.
Joy is a net of love by which
you can catch souls.

MOTHER TERESA

Look at a day when you are supremely satisfied at the end. It is not a day when you lounge around doing nothing; it is when you have had everything to do, and you have done it.

MARGARET THATCHER

*Seize the day, and put the least possible trust in tomorrow.*

HORACE

It is hard to fail, but it is worse
never to have tried to succeed.

THEODORE ROOSEVELT

*The great recipe
for success is to work,
and always work.*

LEON GAMBETTA

Consider the lilies how they grow.

LUKE 12:27 KJV

*I have faith that yields to none.*

Ovid

Nothing is worth
more than this day.

Johann Wolfgang von Goethe

You have achieved success
if you have lived well, laughed
often, and loved much.

UNKNOWN

*Genius is one percent inspiration, ninety-nine percent perspiration.*

THOMAS EDISON

Trust God to move mountains,
but keep on digging.

*OUR DAILY BREAD*

*Who stops being better stops being good.*

Oliver Cromwell

I cannot change the whole world,
but I can change a small part of it.

KAY FLORENTINO

You are part of the great plan,
an indispensable part. You are needed;
you have your own unique share
in the freedom of Creation.

MADELEINE L'ENGLE

*Do not wait to strike till the iron is hot;
but make it hot by striking.*

WILLIAM B. SPRAGUE

When ye pray, believe.

MARK 11:24 KJV

*What you achieve through the journey of life is not as important as who you become.*

UNKNOWN

We are what we repeatedly do. Excellence,
therefore, is not an act but a habit.

ARISTOTLE

Never let the fear of striking
out get in your way.

GEORGE HERMAN "BABE" RUTH

When one door closes, another one opens,
but we often look so long and regretfully
at the closed door that we fail to see
the one that has opened for us.

ALEXANDER GRAHAM BELL

The greatest gift we can give one another is rapt attention to one another's existence.

SUE ATCHLEY EBAUGH

*Self-confidence is the first requisite
to great undertakings.*

SAMUEL JOHNSON

Do not let trifles disturb your tranquility of mind. . . . Life is too precious to be sacrificed for the nonessential and transient. . . . Ignore the inconsequential.

GRENVILLE KLEISER

*Real joy comes not from ease or riches or from the praise of men, but from doing something worthwhile.*

SIR WILFRED GRENFELL

Growth is the only evidence of life.

JOHN H. NEWMAN

The very hairs of your head
are all numbered. Fear ye not
therefore, ye are of more
value than many sparrows.

Matthew 10:30–31 KJV

Experience teaches only the teachable.

ALDOUS HUXLEY

*Thy fate is the common fate of all;*
*Into each life some rain must fall.*

HENRY WADSWORTH LONGFELLOW

Courage is the ladder on which
all the other virtues mount.

CLARE BOOTH LUCE

Leap, and the net will appear.

UNKNOWN

*I cannot give you the formula for success, but I can give you the formula for failure—which is: Try to please everybody.*

HERBERT B. SWOPE

*The man who has confidence in himself gains the confidence of others.*

HASIDIC SAYING

Little faith will bring your soul to heaven, but great faith will bring heaven to your soul.

CHARLES H. SPURGEON

Personality can open doors,
but only character can keep them open.

ELMER G. LETTERMAN

Experience is the mother of truth;
and by experience we learn wisdom.

WILLIAM SHIPPEN JR.

Isn't everything you have and everything you are sheer gifts from God?. . . You already have all you need.

1 Corinthians 4:7–8 msg

People grow through experience if they meet life honestly and courageously. This is how character is built.

ELEANOR ROOSEVELT

Let us have faith that
right makes might.

ABRAHAM LINCOLN

*The greatest satisfaction in life is achieving what everyone said could not be done.*

CHINESE PROVERB

*So divinely is the world organized that every one of us, in our place and time, is in balance with everything else.*

JOHANN WOLFGANG VON GOETHE

I do not pray for success;
I ask for faithfulness.

MOTHER TERESA

Nothing great was ever
achieved without enthusiasm.

RALPH WALDO EMERSON

The reason some [people] do not succeed
is because their wishbone is where
their backbone ought to be.

UNKNOWN

Change is the law of life. And those who look only to the past or present are certain to miss the future.

JOHN F. KENNEDY

I am not afraid of tomorrow,
for I have seen yesterday,
and I love today.

William Allen White

"My Presence will go with you,
and I will give you rest."

EXODUS 33:14 NIV

You see things; and you say "Why?"
But I dream things that never
were; and I say "Why not?"

GEORGE BERNARD SHAW

*Life is a wilderness of twists and turns where faith is your only compass.*

PAUL SANTAGUIDA

Yesterday is gone.
Tomorrow has not yet come.
We have only today. Let us begin.

MOTHER TERESA

You can't try your wings if
you're sitting on the nest.

LISA BEVERE

Take the first step in faith.
You don't have to see the whole
staircase—just take the first step.

MARTIN LUTHER KING JR.

Love comforteth like
sunshine after rain.

WILLIAM SHAKESPEARE

*Within our dreams and aspirations we find our opportunities.*

SUE ATCHLEY EBAUGH

*It is a mistaken idea that greatness and great success mean the same thing.*

UNKNOWN

What I must do is all that concerns me,
not what the people think.

RALPH WALDO EMERSON

Mercy, peace and love
be yours in abundance.

JUDE 1:2 NIV

The future belongs to those who believe in the beauty of their dreams.

UNKNOWN

To have what you want is riches;
but to be able to do without is power.

GEORGE MACDONALD

Choose always the way that seems
best, however rough it may be.

PYTHAGORAS

*All life is an experiment.*
*The more experiments*
*you make, the better.*

RALPH WALDO EMERSON

Simplicity is indeed often the sign of truth and a criterion of beauty.

MAHLON HOAGLAND

Develop success from failures.
Discouragement and failure are two of
the surest stepping-stones to success.

DALE CARNEGIE

*Great works are performed not
by strength but by perseverance.*

SAMUEL JOHNSON

Great ability develops and
reveals itself increasingly
with every new assignment.

BALTASAR GRACIAN

The world of tomorrow belongs
to the person who has
the vision today.

ROBERT SCHULLER

Here is the test to find whether your mission
on earth is finished: If you're alive, it isn't.

RICHARD BACH

With minds that are alert
and fully sober, set your hope fully
on the grace to be brought to you
when Jesus Christ is revealed.

1 PETER 1:13 NIV

There are only two ways to live your life. One is as though nothing is a miracle. The other is as though everything is a miracle.

ALBERT EINSTEIN

But if I knew everything, there would be no wonder, because what I believe is far more than I know.

MADELEINE L'ENGLE

Laughter is the gift of love, the music of the soul, and the essence of humanity.

UNKNOWN

Success is getting what you want.
Happiness is wanting what you get.

DALE CARNEGIE

*Character is what you are in the dark.*

DWIGHT MOODY

The only reward of virtue
is virtue; the only way to
have a friend is to be one.

RALPH WALDO EMERSON

We cannot do great things. . .
only small things with great love.

MOTHER TERESA

*It is only with the heart that one can see rightly. What is essential is invisible to the eye.*

Antoine de Saint-Exupéry

"*He will yet fill your mouth with laughter and your lips with shouts of joy.*"

JOB 8:21 NIV

All along life's broad highway
I found loveliness today.

CARLETON EVERETT KNOX

I am beginning to learn that it is the sweet, simple things of life which are the real ones after all.

LAURA INGALLS WILDER

Never be afraid to trust an
unknown future to a known God.

CORRIE TEN BOOM

*Keep your friendships in repair.*

RALPH WALDO EMERSON

To see a world in a grain of sand
and a heaven in a wild flower,
hold infinity in the palm of your
hand and eternity in an hour.

WILLIAM BLAKE

If you surrender completely to
the moments as they pass, you
live more richly those moments.

ANNE MORROW LINDBERGH

*Love is love's reward.*

JOHN DRYDEN

*The reason birds can fly and we can't is simply that they have perfect faith, for to have faith is to have wings.*

J. M. BARRIE

Shoot for the moon.
Even if you miss, you'll land
among the stars.

LES BROWN

"But I lavish unfailing love
for a thousand generations on those
who love me and obey my commands."

DEUTERONOMY 5:10 NLT

If you can imagine it, you can
achieve it. If you can dream it,
you can become it.

WILLIAM ARTHUR WARD

Respect is love in plain clothes.

FRANKIE BYRNE

*Look at life through the
windshield, not the
rearview mirror.*

BYRD BAGGETT

We must never be afraid to go too far,
for success lies just beyond.

MARCEL PROUST

Write it on your heart that every day
is the best day in the year.

RALPH WALDO EMERSON

Feed your faith, and your doubts will starve to death.

*Our Daily Bread*

Whoever is happy will make others happy, too. He who has courage and faith will never perish in misery.

ANNE FRANK

Worry is interest paid on
trouble before it falls due.

W. R. INGE

The seed of joy grows
best in a field of peace.

ROBERT J. WICKS

Because of Christ and our faith
in him, we can now come boldly
and confidently into God's presence.

EPHESIANS 3:12 NLT

Life is a series of surprises.

RALPH WALDO EMERSON

Nothing is really work unless you would rather be doing something else.

J. M. BARRIE

Life is either a daring adventure or nothing.

HELEN KELLER

Do what you can, with what
you have, where you are.

THEODORE ROOSEVELT

*Innocence is like polished armor; it adorns and defends.*

BISHOP ROBERT SOUTH

*Time wasted is existence; used, is life.*

EDWARD YOUNG

It is better to have nobility of character than nobility of birth.

The things we think on are the things that feed our souls. If we think on pure and lovely things, we shall grow pure and lovely like them.

HANNAH WHITALL SMITH

Experience is a jewel.

WILLIAM SHAKESPEARE

*Love never gives up, never loses faith,*
*is always hopeful, and endures through*
*every circumstance. . . . Love will last forever.*

1 CORINTHIANS 13:7–8 NLT

To love abundantly is to
live abundantly, and to love
forever is to live forever.

UNKNOWN

Big doesn't necessarily mean better.
Sunflowers aren't better than violets.

EDNA FERBER

Your thoughts are building
your life—hourly, daily. Your
thoughts are what your destiny is.

Unknown

[Love] is the divine vitality that everywhere produces and restores life. To each and every one of us, it gives the power of working miracles if we will.

Lydia Maria Child

*I have learned to live each day*
*as it comes and not to borrow*
*trouble by dreading tomorrow.*

DOROTHY DIX

Be patient with everyone, but above all with thyself. I mean, do not be disheartened by your imperfections, but always rise up with fresh courage.

FRANCIS DE SALES

Anybody can sympathize with the sufferings of a friend, but it requires a very fine nature to sympathize with a friend's success.

OSCAR WILDE

Belief is truth held in the mind;
faith is a fire in the heart.

JOSEPH FORT NEWTON

*Yes, you can be a dreamer and a doer, too, if you will remove one word from your vocabulary: impossible.*

ROBERT SCHULLER

Encourage one another daily, as long as it is called "Today". . . . We have come to share in Christ, if indeed we hold our original conviction firmly to the very end.

HEBREWS 3:13–14 NIV

While our hearts are pure,
our lives are happy
and our peace is sure.

WILLIAM WINTER

*God alone is the source
of all true serenity.*

Ellyn Sanna

The best and most beautiful things in
the world cannot be seen or even touched.
They must be felt with the heart.

HELEN KELLER

Friendship is one of the sweetest joys of life.
Many might have failed beneath the bitterness
of their trial had they not found a friend.

CHARLES H. SPURGEON

There are two ways of spreading light: to be the candle or the mirror that reflects it.

EDITH WHARTON

The supreme happiness of life is the conviction of being loved for yourself, or more correctly, being loved in spite of yourself.

VICTOR HUGO

*We are all pencils in the hand
of a writing God, who is sending
love letters to the world.*

MOTHER TERESA

I am only one, but I am still one;
I cannot do everything, but I can
still do something; and because I
cannot do everything, I will not refuse
to do the something that I can do.

EDWARD EVERETT HALE

Trouble shared is trouble halved.

DOROTHY SAYERS

I look behind me and you're there, then up ahead and you're there, too—your reassuring presence, coming and going. This is too much, too wonderful—I can't take it all in!

PSALM 139:5–6 MSG

*Angels fly because they take themselves lightly.*

UNKNOWN

*Don't put off for tomorrow what you can do today, because if you enjoy it today, you can do it again tomorrow.*

JAMES A. MICHENER

We find in life exactly
what we put into it.

RALPH WALDO EMERSON

Wisdom is knowing what to do next. Skill is knowing how to do it. Virtue is doing it.

THOMAS JEFFERSON

*Goodness is the only investment that never fails.*

HENRY DAVID THOREAU

*Work first, then rest.*

JOHN RUSKIN

What lies behind us and what lies before us are tiny matters compared to what lies within us.

Ralph Waldo Emerson

Still round the corner there may
wait, a new road, or a secret gate.

J. R. R. TOLKIEN

*Our greatest glory consists not in never falling, but in rising every time we fall.*

OLIVER GOLDSMITH

But seek ye first the kingdom of God, and his righteousness; and all these things shall be added unto you.

MATTHEW 6:33 KJV

To have joy one must
share it—happiness
was born a twin.

LORD BYRON

Love is, above all, the gift of oneself.

JEAN ANOUILH

*The future is something which everyone reaches at the rate of sixty minutes an hour, whatever he does, whoever he is.*

C. S. Lewis

*Let us be grateful to people who make us happy; they are the charming gardeners who make our souls bloom.*

MARCEL PROUST

When doubts come, meet them, not with arguments, but with assertions of faith.

HANNAH WHITALL SMITH

God has given us two hands—one to
receive with and the other to give with.
We are not cisterns made for hoarding;
we are channels made for sharing.

BILLY GRAHAM

*Luck marches with those who give their very best.*

H. JACKSON BROWN JR.

Commitment unlocks the doors
of imagination, allows vision,
and gives us the "right stuff"
to turn our dreams into reality.

JAMES WOMACK

*We aim high above the mark to hit the mark.*

RALPH WALDO EMERSON

"For I know the plans I have for you," declares the LORD, "plans to prosper you and not to harm you, plans to give you hope and a future."

JEREMIAH 29:11 NIV

Hope springs exulting on triumphant wing.

ROBERT BURNS

Hand grasps hand, eye lights eye. . .
And great hearts expand, and grow.

ROBERT BROWNING

Resolve to see the world on the sunny side, and you have almost won the battle of life at the outset.

Sir Roger L'Estrange

Where there is great love
there are always miracles.

WILLA CATHER

Each dawn holds a new hope
for a new plan, making the start
of each day the start of a new life.

When you have laboriously
accomplished your daily tasks,
go to sleep in peace. God is awake.

VICTOR HUGO

When I am delivering my
very best, that is when
I feel successful.

ART FETTIG

Hide not your talents.
They for use were made.
What's a sundial in the shade?

BENJAMIN FRANKLIN

*By perseverance, the snail reached the ark.*

CHARLES H. SPURGEON

"The joy of the LORD is your strength!"

NEHEMIAH 8:10 NLT

Success seems to be largely
a matter of hanging on
after others have let go.

WILLIAM FEATHER

Hope quickens all the still parts
of life and keeps the mind awake.

JOSEPH ADDISON

*Courage is the capacity to go ahead in spite of the fear.*

SCOTT PECK

*Great opportunities to help
others seldom come, but
small ones surround us daily.*

SALLY KOCH

A loving heart is the truest wisdom.

CHARLES DICKENS

Keep your feet on the ground, but let your heart soar as high as it will. Refuse to be average or to surrender to the chill of your spiritual environment.

A. W. TOZER

To live is so startling, it leaves
little time for anything else.

EMILY DICKINSON

*[She] who has a why to live
can bear almost any how.*

FRIEDRICH NIETZSCHE

The secret to success is to do the common things uncommonly well.

JOHN D. ROCKEFELLER

May the God of hope fill you will all
joy and peace as you trust in him,
so that you may overflow with hope
by the power of the Holy Spirit.

ROMANS 15:13 NIV

*No act of kindness, no matter how small, is ever wasted.*

AESOP

*I have a simple philosophy:
Fill what's empty. Empty what's
full. Scratch where it itches.*

ALICE ROOSEVELT LONGWORTH

The great use of life is
to spend it for something
that will outlast it.

WILLIAM JAMES

What joy is better than the news of friends?

Robert Browning

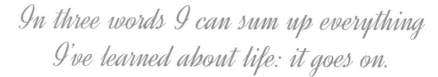

*In three words I can sum up everything
I've learned about life: it goes on.*

ROBERT FROST

*They can conquer
who believe they can.*

RALPH WALDO EMERSON

Your happiness comes from within you, not from the money you make, the trips you take, or the things you own.

FAITH STEWART

It is not length of life,
but depth of life.

RALPH WALDO EMERSON

You will find, as you look back
upon your life, that the moments
when you have really lived
are the moments when you have
done things in the spirit of love.

HENRY DRUMMOND

God is able to bless you abundantly,
so that in all things at all times,
having all that you need,
you will abound in every good work.

2 CORINTHIANS 9:8 NIV

*Life is change. Growth is optional. Choose wisely.*

KAREN KAISER CLARK

If A equals success, then the formula is: A = X + Y + Z. X is work. Y is play. Z is keep your mouth shut.

ALBERT EINSTEIN

No one can make you feel inferior
without your consent.

ELEANOR ROOSEVELT

Keep your face to the sunshine
and you cannot see the shadow.

HELEN KELLER

I will take time to notice the
good things when they come.
I will fix my mind on what
is pure and lovely and upright.

ANITA CORRINE DONIHUE

I never did anything worth doing by accident, nor did any of my inventions come by accident; they came by work.

THOMAS EDISON

*Unbeing dead isn't being alive.*

E. E. CUMMINGS

*Vision without action is a daydream.*
*Action without vision is a nightmare.*

JAPANESE PROVERB

Most people are about as happy as they make up their minds to be.

ABRAHAM LINCOLN

"*Worship the Lord your God and only the Lord your God. Serve him with absolute single-heartedness.*"

LUKE 4:8 MSG

The purpose of life is a life of purpose.

ROBERT BYRNE